GREETING CARD SKETCH BOOK

Jacqueline E. Kelley

Dedicated

To those who have vivid imaginations, who desire to, design Greeting cards.

No part of this book may be reproduced only by permission from the author.

2018 copyright

USA

What

Will

You

Imagine?

7

Imagining beauty in others and a heart of gratitude

For them

Creating a card expressing

"LOVE" IS AWESOME!

Hope you had

Fun

Designing Greeting

Cards

Love y'all

God Bless!

Jacqueline E. Kelley

www.ingramcontent.com/pod-product-compliance
Lightning Source LLC
Chambersburg PA
CBHW062325220526
45469CB00008B/2622